Health (

Teacher's Guide

CONTENTS

Editor: Alan Christopherson, M.S.

Alpha Omega Publications

Published by Alpha Omega Publications, Inc.
300 North McKemy Avenue, Chandler, Arizona 85226-2618

Health Quest

Curriculum Overview

Health Quest

PHYSICAL HEALTH
- Body building blocks
- Body framework
- Body systems
- Growth & development

MENTAL HEALTH
- Thinking & learning
- Emotional disorders
- Social health
- Personal hygiene

NUTRITION
- Nutrients & metabolism
- Basic food groups
- Physical fitness
- Good eating habits

INJURY & DISEASE
- Safety & accidents
- Natural disasters
- Emergency care
- Disease & prevention

STEWARDSHIP
- Environment & health
- Use & misuse of drugs
- Alcohol & alcoholism
- Smoking

Health Quest

LIFEPAC Management

STRUCTURE OF THE HEALTH QUEST CURRICULUM

The Health Quest LIFEPAC curriculum is conveniently structured to provide one teacher handbook containing teacher support material with answer keys and five student worktexts. The worktext format of the Health Quest LIFEPACs allows the student to read the textual information and complete workbook activities all in the same booklet.

Each LIFEPAC is divided into 3 sections and begins with an introduction or overview of the booklet as well as a series of specific learning objectives to give a purpose to the study of the LIFEPAC. The introduction and objectives are followed by a vocabulary section. Vocabulary words are used to develop word recognition. The student should learn all vocabulary words before working the LIFEPAC sections to improve comprehension, retention, and reading skills.

Each activity or written assignment has a number for easy identification, such as 1.1. The first number corresponds to the LIFEPAC section and the number to the right of the decimal is the number of the activity.

Adult checkpoints, which are essential to maintain quality learning, are found at various locations throughout the LIFEPAC. The adult should check 1) neatness of work and penmanship, 2) quality of understanding (tested with a short oral quiz), 3) thoroughness of answers (complete sentences and paragraphs, correct spelling, etc.), 4) completion of activities (no blank spaces), and 5) accuracy of answers as compared to the answer key (all answers correct).

The self test questions are also number coded for easy reference. For example, 2.015 means that this is the 15th question in the self test of Section II. The first number corresponds to the LIFEPAC section, the zero indicates that it is a self test question, and the number to the right of the zero the question number.

The LIFEPAC test is packaged at the centerfold of each LIFEPAC. It should be removed and put aside before giving the booklet to the student for study.

Answer and test keys have the same numbering system as the LIFEPACs and appear at the back of this handbook. The student may be given access to the answer keys (not the test keys) under teacher supervision so that he can score his own work.

A thorough study of the Curriculum Overview by the teacher before instruction begins is essential to the success of the student. The teacher should become familiar with expected skill mastery. The teacher should also preview the objectives that appear at the beginning of each LIFEPAC for additional preparation and planning.

TEST SCORING and GRADING

Answer keys and test keys give examples of correct answers. Many questions are high level and require thinking and creativity on the part of the student. Each answer should be scored based on whether or not the main idea written by the student matches the model example. "Any Order" or "Either Order" in a key indicates that no particular order is necessary to be correct.

Most self tests and LIFEPAC tests in the Health Quest LIFEPACs are scored at 3 points per answer for the content-based questions and one point per answer for the Scripture memory questions. Further, the total test points will vary; they may not always equal 100 points. They may be 78, 85, 100, 105, etc.

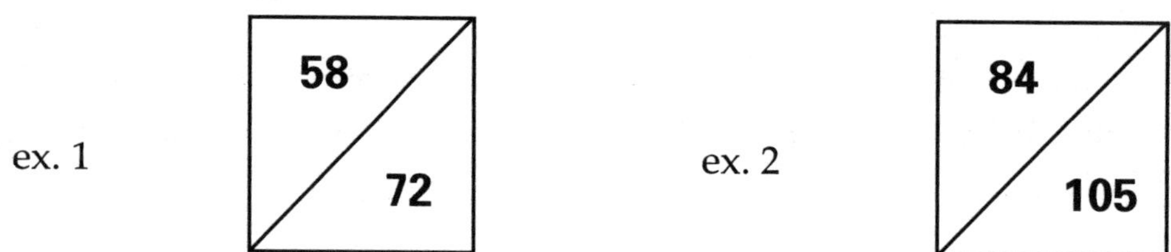

A score box similar to ex.1 above is located at the end of each self test and on the front of the LIFEPAC test. The bottom score, 72, represents the total number of points possible on the test. The upper score, 58, represents the number of points your student will need to receive an 80% or passing grade. If you wish to establish the exact percentage that your student has achieved, find the total points of his correct answers and divide it by the bottom number (in this case 72.) For example, if your student has a point total of 65, divide 65 by 72 for a grade of 90%. Referring to ex. 2, on a test with a total of 105 possible points, the student would have to receive a minimum of 84 correct points for an 80% or passing grade. If your student has received 93 points, simply divide the 93 by 105 for a percentage grade of 86%. Students who receive a score below 80% should review the LIFEPAC and retest using the appropriate Alternate Test found in the Teacher's Guide.

The following is a guideline to assign letter grades for completed LIFEPACs based on a maximum total score of 100 points.

LIFEPAC Test = 60% of the Total Score (or percent grade)
Self Test = 25% of the Total Score (average percent of self tests)
Reports = 10% or 10* points per LIFEPAC
Oral Work = 5% or 5* points per LIFEPAC
*Determined by the teacher's subjective evaluation of the student's daily work.

Example:

LIFEPAC Test Score	=	92%	92 x .60	= 55 points
Self Test Average	=	90%	90 x .25	= 23 points
Reports				= 8 points
Oral Work				= 4 points
TOTAL POINTS				= 90 points

Grade Scale based on point system:

100	–	94	= A
93	–	86	= B
85	–	77	= C
76	–	70	= D
Below		70	= F

TEACHER HINTS and STUDYING TECHNIQUES

LIFEPAC Activities are written to check the level of understanding of the preceding text. The student may look back to the text as necessary to complete these activities; however, a student should never attempt to do the activities without reading (studying) the text first. Self tests and LIFEPAC tests are never open book tests.

Writing complete answers (paragraphs) to some questions is an integral part of the LIFEPAC Curriculum in all subjects. This builds communication and organization skills, increases understanding and retention of ideas, and helps enforce good penmanship. Complete sentences should be encouraged for this type of activity. Obviously, single words or phrases do not meet the intent of the activity, since multiple lines are given for the response.

Review is essential to student success. Time invested in review where review is suggested will be time saved in correcting errors later. Self tests, unlike the section activities, are closed book. This procedure helps to identify weaknesses before they become too great to overcome. Certain objectives from self tests are cumulative and test previous sections; therefore, good preparation for a self test must include all material studied up to that testing point.

The following procedure checklist has been found to be successful in developing good study habits in the LIFEPAC curriculum.

1. Read the Introduction and Table of Contents.
2. Read the objectives.
3. Recite and study the entire vocabulary (glossary) list.
4. Study each section as follows:
    a. Read all the text for the entire section, but answer none of the activities.

b. Return to the beginning of the section and memorize each vocabulary word and definition.

c. Reread the section, complete the activities, check the answers with the answer key, correct all errors, and have the teacher check.

d. Read the self test but do not answer the questions.

e. Go to the beginning of the first section and reread the text and answers to the activities up to the self test you have not yet done.

f. Answer the questions to the self test without looking back.

g. Have the self test checked by the teacher.

h. Correct the self test and have the teacher check the corrections.

i. Repeat steps a–h for each section.

5. Use the SQ3R* method to prepare for the LIFEPAC test.
6. Take the LIFEPAC test as a closed book test.
7. LIFEPAC tests are administered and scored under direct teacher supervision. Students who receive scores below 80% should review the LIFEPAC using the SQ3R* study method and take the Alternate Test located in the Teacher Handbook. The final test grade may be the grade on the Alternate Test or an average of the grades from the original LIFEPAC test and the Alternate Test.

***SQ3R:** Scan the whole LIFEPAC.
Question yourself on the objectives.
Read the whole LIFEPAC again.
Recite through an oral examination.
Review weak areas.

GOAL SETTING and SCHEDULES

Basically, two factors need to be considered when assigning work to a student in the LIFEPAC curriculum.

The first factor is time. An average of 45 minutes should be devoted to each subject, each day. Remember, this is only an average. Because of extenuating circumstances a student may spend only 15 minutes on a subject one day and the next day spend 90 minutes on the same subject.

The second factor is the number of pages to be worked in each subject. A single LIFEPAC is designed to take 3 to 4 weeks to complete. Allowing about 3-4 days for LIFEPAC introduction, review, and tests, the student has approximately 15 days to complete the LIFEPAC pages. Simply take the number of pages in the LIFEPAC, divide it by 15 and you will have the number of pages that must be completed on a daily basis to keep the student on schedule. For example, a LIFEPAC containing 45 pages will require 3 completed pages per day. Again, this is only an average. While working a 45 page LIFEPAC, the student may complete only 1 page the first day if the text has a lot of activities or reports, but go on to complete 5 pages the next day.

FORMS

The sample weekly lesson plan and student grading sheet forms are included in this section as teacher support materials and may be duplicated at the convenience of the teacher.

The student grading sheet is provided for those who desire to follow the suggested guidelines for assignment of letter grades found on page LM-5 of this section. The student's self test scores should be posted as percentage grades. When the LIFEPAC is completed the teacher should average the self test grades, multiply the average by .25 and post the points in the box marked self test points. The LIFEPAC percentage grade should be multiplied by .60 and posted. Next, the teacher should award and post points for written reports and oral work. A report may be any type of written work assigned to the student whether it is a LIFEPAC or additional learning activity. Oral work includes the student's ability to respond orally to questions which may or may not be related to LIFEPAC activities or any type of oral report assigned by the teacher. The points may then be totaled and a final grade entered along with the date that the LIFEPAC was completed.

The Student Record Book which was specifically designed for use with the Alpha Omega curriculum provides space to record weekly progress for one student over a nine-week period as well as a place to post self test and LIFEPAC scores. The Student Record Books are available through the current Alpha Omega catalog; however, unlike the enclosed forms these books are not for duplication and should be purchased in sets of four to cover a full academic year.

WEEKLY LESSON PLANNER

Week of:

	Subject	Subject	Subject	Subject
Monday				
	Subject	Subject	Subject	Subject
Tuesday				
	Subject	Subject	Subject	Subject
Wednesday				
	Subject	Subject	Subject	Subject
Thursday				
	Subject	Subject	Subject	Subject
Friday				

WEEKLY LESSON PLANNER

Week of:

	Subject	Subject	Subject	Subject
Monday				
	Subject	Subject	Subject	Subject
Tuesday				
	Subject	Subject	Subject	Subject
Wednesday				
	Subject	Subject	Subject	Subject
Thursday				
	Subject	Subject	Subject	Subject
Friday				

Student Name ______________________ Year ________

Health Quest

LP #	Self Test Scores by Sections 1	2	3	4	5	Self Test Points	LIFEPAC Test	Oral Points	Report Points	Final Grade	Date
01											
02											
03											
04											
05											

Student Name ______________________ Year ________

Health Quest

LP #	Self Test Scores by Sections 1	2	3	4	5	Self Test Points	LIFEPAC Test	Oral Points	Report Points	Final Grade	Date
01											
02											
03											
04											
05											

Student Name ______________________ Year ________

Health Quest

LP #	Self Test Scores by Sections 1	2	3	4	5	Self Test Points	LIFEPAC Test	Oral Points	Report Points	Final Grade	Date
01											
02											
03											
04											
05											

Student Name ______________________ Year ________

Health Quest

LP #	Self Test Scores by Sections 1	2	3	4	5	Self Test Points	LIFEPAC Test	Oral Points	Report Points	Final Grade	Date
01											
02											
03											
04											
05											

Health Quest

Teacher Notes

HEALTH QUEST PENTATHLON THEME

The Health Quest Pentathlon theme is set along the roadway/track of life and sets before the student five challenges similar to the Olympic Pentathlon. Each Health Quest LIFEPAC begins a new health challenge. Students are given a variety of activities that address learning style preferences (visual, auditory, kinesthetic learners) as well as activity preferences.

Built-in application exercises encourage critical thinking, enabling students to confidently evaluate health alternatives and make wise decisions in life.

HEALTH QUEST PENTATHLON POSTER

The Health Quest Pentathlon Poster (shown on the following page) is a 22″ x 34″ full-color poster that corresponds to completion of Health Quest Pentathlon (HQP) activities at the end of each section of the Health Quest LIFEPACs. There are three sections per LIFEPAC with approximately three HQP activities per section. When the student completes all of the HQP activities (or any alternate activities the parent/teacher should choose), he or she is awarded a gold medal sticker to place in the appropriate location on the Health Quest Pentathlon poster. Each Pentathlon event has a place for three gold stickers. Students earn a total of 15 gold stickers to complete their circuit around the Health Quest Pentathlon Track.

The HQP activities are explained in each LIFEPAC and can be modified as the parent/teacher desires.

HEALTH QUEST SCRIPTURE MEMORY ACTIVITIES

Each Health Quest LIFEPAC includes a Scripture passage for memorization. The King James Version (KJV) has been used for these Scripture memory exercises.

This Teacher's Guide includes Scripture memory activities in the King James Version of the Bible and includes KJV text and answer keys for each of these activities.

INSTRUCTIONS FOR THE HEALTH QUEST CURRICULUM

The Health Quest curriculum is structured so that the daily instructional material is written directly into the LIFEPACs. The student is encouraged to read and follow this instructional material in order to develop independent study habits. The teacher should introduce the LIFEPAC to the student, set a required completion schedule, complete teacher checks, be available for questions regarding both content and procedures, administer and grade tests, and develop additional learning activities as desired. Teachers working with several students may schedule their time so that students are assigned to a quiet work activity when it is necessary to spend instructional time with one particular student.

HEALTH QUEST
Pentathlon
Building Healthy Lifestyles for the Glory of God
Start here
FINISH
1
Congratulations! You've completed the **HQP Activities for Section I.** Place your gold medal sticker here.
Congratulations! You've completed the **HQP Activities for Section II.** Place your gold medal sticker here.
Congratulations! You've completed the **HQP Activities for Section III.** Place your gold medal sticker here.
2
Congratulations! You've completed the **HQP Activities for Section I.** Place your gold medal sticker here.
Congratulations! You've completed the **HQP Activities for Section II.** Place your gold medal sticker here.
Congratulations! You've completed the **HQP Activities for Section III.** Place your gold medal sticker here.
3
Congratulations! You've completed the **HQP Activities for Section I.** Place your gold medal sticker here.
Congratulations! You've completed the **HQP Activities for Section II.** Place your gold medal sticker here.
Congratulations! You've completed the **HQP Activities for Section III.** Place your gold medal sticker here.
4
Congratulations! You've completed the **HQP Activities for Section I.** Place your gold medal sticker here.
Congratulations! You've completed the **HQP Activities for Section II.** Place your gold medal sticker here.
Congratulations! You've completed the **HQP Activities for Section III.** Place your gold medal sticker here.
5
Congratulations! You've completed the **HQP Activities for Section I.** Place your gold medal sticker here.
Congratulations! You've completed the **HQP Activities for Section II.** Place your gold medal sticker here.
Congratulations! You've completed the **HQP Activities for Section III.** Place your gold medal sticker here.

COURSE OBJECTIVES AND CONSIDERATIONS

Course Objectives

Health Quest Pentathlon has been developed as an upper elementary Health course to accomplish the following objectives:

1. The students will gain an awareness of health as it applies personally to their own bodies, mind and emotions as well as generally in their living environment, community and world.
2. The students will learn to identify the components of a healthy lifestyle and set reasonable goals to achieve a lifestyle of wellness.
3. The students will grow to understand that good health is a life long pursuit.
4. The students will receive continuous opportunity and motivation to apply health principles in their everyday lives participating in the Health Course theme, "Health Quest Pentathlon."
5. The students will become aware that incorporating sound health practices engender a lifestyle of moderation and wellness.
6. The students will grow in understanding their responsibility to properly steward the bodies God has given them as directed in the Bible.
7. The students will gain appreciation of health as it applies to the broader society and world and their responsibility to engender good health around them.

Course Considerations

This course has been developed to establish lifelong good health habits and in consideration of the pre-teen students:

1. Expanding awareness about their changing bodies
2. Growing susceptibility to health fads, trends and unhealthy lifestyles
3. Maturing ability to incorporate health living steps into their own lifestyle to avoid injury and disease
4. Developing aptitude to apply material they learn into their own lives and the surrounding environment.
5. Broadening concern of health as it applies to the environment, their community and the world around them.

ADDITIONAL RESOURCES TO AUGMENT LEARNING

Many other health resources exist which would benefit students and educators in studying the topics covered in the Health Quest Pentathlon.

Organizations

These will often allow field trips and/or provide on-site group presentations as well as handouts.

Adopt-A-Highway Program (contact your state's Department of Transportation)
American Red Cross
Community Action Center (providing relief to underprivileged)
Department of Public Safety
Hospital/Emergency Medical Services
Local Fire Department
Local Poison Control Center
Local Volunteer Center
National Response Center (toxic chemicals and oil spills)

Health-Related Web-sites

While not exhaustive, this list should provide links to many other valuable sites. Many of these sites offer to send materials.

www.cancer.org American Cancer Society (healthful living)

www.ada.org American Dental Association (healthy teeth)

ww.amhrt.org American Heart Association (healthful living)

www.ama-assn.org/ American Medical Association (physician/patient relationship)

www.redcross.org American Red Cross (first aid, first aid supplies, handling crises)

www.cdc.gov Centers for Disease Control and Prevention

www.epa.gov Environmental Protection Agency (community and environmental health)

www.fda.gov Food and Drug Administration

www.radix.net/~mschelling/health.html Health-related Web-sites

www.nalusda.gov/homepage.html National Agriculture Library (nutrition)

www.dairyinfo.com National Dairy Council (nutrition)

www.nscl.org National Safety Council (safety, injury and violence)

www.usda.gov USDA (nutrition, Food Pyramid)

HEALTH QUEST PENTATHLON SOURCES USED

Hough, Heidi, ed. *The American Medical Association Home Medical Encyclopedia.* New York: Random House, 1989.

Gray, Henry. *Gray's Anatomy.* New York: Bounty Books, 1975.

American Red Cross Standard First Aid: Workbook. American Red Cross, 1988.

Encarta Encyclopedia. Microsoft, 1997.

Funk and Wagnalls Encyclopedia. Funk and Wagnalls, 1994.

ADDITIONAL RESOURCES

Owen, Jim, *Christian Psychology's War on God's Word.* Santa Barbara, CA: EastGate Publishers, 1993.

Adams, Jay E., *Competent to Counsel.* Grand Rapids, MI, Zondervan Publishing House, 1970.

Williamson, G.I., *Westminster Confession of Faith: A Study Manual.* Phillipsburg, NJ: Presbyterian and Reformed Publishing, 1989.

Health Quest

King James Version
Scripture Memory Exercises

Answer Keys
Self Test Keys
LIFEPAC Test Keys
Alternate Test Keys

PSALM 139 (King James Version)

1 O Lord, thou hast searched me, and known me.

2 Thou knowest my downsitting and mine uprising, thou understandest my thought afar off.

3 Thou compassest my path and my lying down, and art acquainted with all my ways.

4 For there is not a word in my tongue, but, lo, O Lord, thou knowest it altogether.

5 Thou hast beset me behind and before, and laid thine hand upon me.

6 Such knowledge is too wonderful for me; it is high, I cannot attain unto it.

7 Whither shall I go from thy spirit? or whither shall I flee from thy presence?

8 If I ascend up into heaven, thou art there: if I make my bed in hell, behold, thou art there.

9 If I take the wings of the morning, and dwell in the uttermost parts of the sea;

10 Even there shall thy hand lead me, and thy right hand shall hold me.

11 If I say, Surely the darkness shall cover me; even the night shall be light about me.

12 Yea, the darkness hideth not from thee; but the night shineth as the day: the darkness and the light are both alike to thee.

13 For thou hast possessed my reins: thou hast covered me in my mother's womb.

14 I will praise thee; for I am fearfully and wonderfully made: marvellous are thy works; and that my soul knoweth right well.

15 My substance was not hid from thee, when I was made in secret, and curiously wrought in the lowest parts of the earth.

16 Thine eyes did see my substance, yet being unperfect; and in thy book all my members were written, which in continuance were fashioned, when as yet there was none of them.

17 How precious also are thy thoughts unto me, O God! how great is the sum of them!

18 If I should count them, they are more in number than the sand: when I awake, I am still with thee.

19 Surely thou wilt slay the wicked, O God: depart from me therefore, ye bloody men.

20 For they speak against thee wickedly, and thine enemies take thy name in vain.

21 Do not I hate them, O Lord, that hate thee? and am not I grieved with those that rise up against thee?

22 I hate them with perfect hatred: I count them mine enemies.

23 Search me, O God, and know my heart: try me, and know my thoughts:

24 And see if there be any wicked way in me, and lead me in the way everlasting.

COLOSSIANS 3:1–13 (King James Version)

1 If ye then be risen with Christ, seek those things which are above, where Christ sitteth on the right hand of God.

2 Set your affection on things above, not on things on the earth.

3 For ye are dead, and your life is hid with Christ in God.

4 When Christ, who is our life, shall appear, then shall ye also appear with him in glory.

5 Mortify therefore your members which are upon the earth; fornication, uncleanness, inordinate affection, evil concupiscence, and covetousness, which is idolatry:

6 For which things' sake the wrath of God cometh on the children of disobedience:

7 In the which ye also walked sometime, when ye lived in them.

8 But now ye also put off all these; anger, wrath, malice, blasphemy, filthy communication out of your mouth.

9 Lie not one to another, seeing that ye have put off the old man with his deeds;

10 And have put on the new man, which is renewed in knowledge after the image of him that created him:

11 Where there is neither Greek nor Jew, circumcision nor uncircumcision, Barbarian, Scythian, bond nor free: but Christ is all, and in all.

12 Put on therefore, as the elect of God, holy and beloved, bowels of mercies, kindness, humbleness of mind, meekness, longsuffering;

13 Forbearing one another, and forgiving one another, if any man have a quarrel against any: even as Christ forgave you, so also do ye.

I CORINTHIANS 6:12–13 & 19–20 (King James Version)

12 All things are lawful unto me, but all things are not expedient: all things are lawful for me, but I will not be brought under the power of any.

13 Meats for the belly, and the belly for meats: but God shall destroy both it and them. Now the body is not for fornication, but for the Lord; and the Lord for the body.

19 What? know ye not that your body is the temple of the Holy Ghost which is in you, which ye have of God, and ye are not your own?

20 For ye are bought with a price: therefore glorify God in your body, and in your spirit, which are God's.

LUKE 10:30–37 (King James Version)

30 And Jesus answering said, A certain man went down from Jerusalem to Jericho, and fell among thieves, which stripped him of his raiment, and wounded him, and departed, leaving him half dead.

31 And by chance there came down a certain priest that way: and when he saw him, he passed by on the other side.

32 And likewise a Levite, when he was at the place, came and looked on him, and passed by on the other side.

33 But a certain Samaritan, as he journeyed, came where he was: and when he saw him, he had compassion on him,

34 And went to him, and bound up his wounds, pouring in oil and wine, and set him on his own beast, and brought him to an inn, and took care of him.

35 And on the morrow when he departed, he took out two pence, and gave them to the host, and said unto him, Take care of him; and whatsoever thou spendest more, when I come again, I will repay thee.

36 Which now of these three, thinkest thou, was neighbour unto him that fell among the thieves?

37 And he said, He that shewed mercy on him. Then said Jesus unto him, Go, and do thou likewise.

GENESIS 1:26–31 (King James Version)

26 And God said, Let us make man in our
image, after our likeness: and let them
have dominion over the fish of the sea,
and over the fowl of the air, and over
the cattle, and over all the earth, and
over every creeping thing that creepeth
upon the earth.

27 So God created man in his own image,
in the image of God created he him;
male and female created he them.

28 And God blessed them, and God said
unto them, Be fruitful, and multiply,
and replenish the earth, and subdue it:
and have dominion over the fish of the
sea, and over the fowl of the air, and
over every living thing that moveth
upon the earth.

29 And God said, Behold, I have given you
every herb bearing seed, which is upon
the face of all the earth, and every tree,
in the which is the fruit of a tree
yielding seed; to you it shall be for
meat.

30 And to every beast of the earth, and to
every fowl of the air, and to every thing
that creepeth upon the earth, wherein
there is life, I have given every green
herb for meat: and it was so.

31 And God saw every thing that he had
made, and, behold, it was very good.
And the evening and the morning were
the sixth day.

Complete Psalm 139:1–16.

1.1 O Lord, thou hast searched me, and __________ me.
Thou knowest my __________ and mine __________,
thou understandest my thought afar off.
Thou compassest my __________ and my lying __________, and
art acquainted with all my __________.
For there is not a __________ in my __________, but, lo, O
Lord, thou __________ it altogether.
Thou hast __________ me behind and __________, and
__________ thine __________ upon me.
Such knowledge is too __________ for me; it is __________,
I cannot attain unto it.
Whither shall I go from thy __________? or whither shall I
__________ from thy presence?
If I ascend up into __________, thou art there: if I make my
__________ in __________, behold, thou art there.
If I take the __________ of the morning, and dwell in the
__________ parts of the __________;
Even there shall thy __________ lead me, and thy __________
hand shall hold me.
If I say, Surely the __________ shall cover me; even the
__________ shall be __________ about me.
Yea, the darkness __________ not from thee; but the
__________ shineth as the day: the __________ and
the __________ are both alike to thee.
For thou hast __________ my reins: thou hast covered me in
my __________ __________.
I will praise thee; for I am __________ and wonderfully made:
__________ are thy works; and that my __________
knoweth right well.
My __________ was not hid from thee, when I was made
in __________, and __________ wrought in the
lowest parts of the earth.

Thine eyes did see my substance, yet being ______________________;
and in thy ______________ all my members were __________________,
which in continuance were fashioned, when as yet there was
______________ of ______________.

SELF TEST 1

Fill in the blanks (each answer, 1 point).

Psalm 139:13–16:

1.026 For thou hast ______________________ my reins: thou hast covered me in my
mother's ______________________.
I will praise thee; for I am ______________________ and wonderfully made:
______________________ are thy works; and that my soul knoweth right well.
My ______________________ was not hid from thee, when I was made
in ______________________, and ______________________ wrought in the
lowest parts of the ______________________. Thine eyes did see my
substance, yet being ______________________; and in thy book all my
members were ______________________, which in
______________________ were fashioned, when as yet there was
______________________ of them.

3.36 In this first Health Quest LIFEPAC you've become aware of just a few of the complex parts of your human body. No wonder David wrote in Psalm 139:13–16

For thou hast possessed my reins:
thou hast covered me in my mother's womb.
I will praise thee; for I am fearfully and wonderfully made:
marvellous are thy works;
and that my soul knoweth right well.
My substance was not hid from thee,
when I was made in secret,
and curiously wrought in the lowest parts of the earth.
Thine eyes did see my substance, yet being unperfect;
and in thy book all my members were written,
which in continuance were fashioned,
when as yet there was none of them.

Memorize and recite these verses to an adult.

LIFEPAC TEST 1

41. **Fill in the blanks from Psalm 139:13–16** (each answer, 1 point).

For thou hast ____________________ my reins: thou hast covered me in my ____________________ ____________________. I will ____________________ thee; for I am ____________________ and ____________________ made: ____________________ are thy works; and that my ____________________ knoweth right well. My ____________________ was not ____________ from thee, when I was made in ____________________, and ____________________ ____________________ in the ____________________ parts of the ____________________. Thine eyes did see my ____________________, yet being ____________________; and in thy ____________________ all my members were written, which in continuance were ____________________, when as yet there were ____________________ of them.

Complete Colossians 3:1–13

1.1 If ye then be ____________ with Christ, seek those things which are above, where Christ sitteth on the right ____________ of God.

Set your ________________ on things above, not on things on the earth.

For ye are dead, and your ____________ is hid with Christ in God.

When Christ, who is our life, shall ________________ , then shall ye also appear with Him in glory.

__________________ therefore your members which are upon the ________________; fornication, uncleanness, inordinate ________________ , evil concupiscence, and covetousness, which is ____________________ :

For which things' sake the ______________ of God cometh upon the children of ____________________ :

In the which ye also ________________ some time, when ye lived in them.

But now ye also put off all these; ____________ , wrath, malice, blasphemy, ______________ communication out of your ______________ .

___________ not one to __________________ , seeing that ye have put off the old man with his deeds;

And have put on the new ____________ , which is renewed in ____________________ after the image of him that ________________ him:

Where there is neither Greek nor ____________ , circumcision nor uncircumcision, Barbarian, Scythian, ____________ nor free: but Christ is all, and in all.

Put on therefore, as the elect of ____________ , holy and beloved, bowels of ______________ , kindness, humbleness of mind, ______________ , longsuffering;

Forbearing one another, and ________________ one another, if any man have a ______________ against any: even as Christ forgave you, so you also do ye.

SELF TEST 1

Fill in the blanks with the correct word (each answer, 1 point).

Colossians 3:5–8:

1.018 ____________ therefore your ____________ which are upon the earth; fornication, ____________, inordinate affection, evil concupiscence, and ____________, which is ____________: For which things' sake the ____________ of God ____________ on the children of ____________: In the which ____________ also ____________ some time when ye ____________ in them. But now ye also must put off all these; ____________, wrath, ____________ blasphemy, ____________ communication out of your mouth.

Colossians 3:12–13:

Put on therefore, as the ____________ of ____________, holy and ____________, bowels of ____________, kindness, humbleness of mind, meekness, ____________; Forbearing one ____________, and ____________ one another, if any man have a ____________ against any: even as ____________ forgave you, so also do ye."

2.43 Memorize Colossians 3:8–10, 12–13 and recite it to a parent or teacher.

"But now ye also put off all these; anger, wrath, malice, blasphemy, filthy communication out of your mouth.

Lie not one to another, seeing that ye have put off the old man with his deeds;

And have put on the new man, which is renewed in knowledge after the image of him that created him:

Put on therefore, as the elect of God, holy and beloved, bowels of mercies, kindness, humbleness of mind, meekness, longsuffering;

Forbearing one another, and forgiving one another, if any man have a quarrel against any: even as Christ forgave you, so also do ye."

SELF TEST 2

Complete Colossians 3:8–10 and 12–13 (each answer, 1 point).

2.026 But now ye also put off all these: anger, ________________, malice, blasphemy, ______________ communication out of your mouth. ____________ not one to another, seeing that ye have put off the old man with his ______________; And have put on the new man, which is renewed in ______________________ after the image of __________ that created him.

Put on therefore, as the ______________ of God, ________________ and beloved, bowels of ______________, kindness, humbleness of mind, meekness, _______________________; Forbearing one another, and _________________ one another, if any man have a ____________________ against any: even as Christ _____________________ you, so also do ye.

SELF TEST 3

Complete these verses from Colossians 3:5–8 and 12–13 (each answer, 1 point).

3.026 Mortify therefore your ________________ which are upon the earth; fornication, uncleanness, inordinate affection, ________________ concupiscence, and ________________, which is idolatry: For which things' sake the ________________ of God cometh on the children of ________________ : In the which ye also ________________ sometime, when ye lived in them. But now ye also put off all these: ________________, wrath, malice, blasphemy, ________________ communication out of your mouth.

Put on therefore, as the elect of ________________, holy and ________________, bowels of mercies, ________________, humbleness of mind, ________________, longsuffering; Forbearing one another, and ________________ one another, if any man have a quarrel against any: even as ________________ forgave you, so also do ye.

LIFEPAC TEST 2

Complete the following verses from Colossians 3:5–8, 12,13 (each answer, 1 point).

30. ________________ therefore your ________________ which are upon the earth; fornication, uncleanness, inordinate affection, evil concupiscence, and ________________, which is idolatry: For which things' sake the ________________ of God cometh on the children of ________________: In the which ye also walked some time, when ye lived in them. But now ye also put off all these; ________________, wrath, ________________, blasphemy, filthy communication out of your mouth.

    Put on therefore, as the elect of God, holy and ________________, bowels of ________________, kindness, humbleness of mind, meekness, longsuffering; Forbearing one another, and ________________ one another, if any man have a quarrel against any: even as ________________ forgave you, so also do ye.

Complete I Corinthians 6:12–13 and 19–20.

1.1 All things are ____________________ unto me, but all things are not expedient: all things are ____________________ for me, but I will not be brought under the power of any. Meats for the ____________________ and the belly for meats, but God shall ____________________ both it and them. Now the body is not for ____________________, but for the ____________________; and the Lord for the body.

What? know ye not that your __________________ is the temple of the ______________ ________________ which is in you, which ye have of ____________, and ye are not your_______________? For ye are ____________________ with a price: therefore ____________________ God in your body and in your ____________________, which are God's.

SELF TEST 1

Fill in the blanks with the correct word (each answer, 1 point).

1.021 **I Corinthians 6:12–13 and 19–20:**

All things are ____________________ unto me, but all things are not expedient: All things are lawful for me, but I will not be brought under the ________________ of any. Meats for the belly, and the belly for meats: but ________________ shall ____________________ both it and them. Now the ________________ is not for fornication, but for the ________________ ;and the Lord for the body.

What? know ye not that your body is the ________________ of the Holy Ghost, which is in you, which ye have of ______________, and ye are not your own? For ye are _____________________ with a ________________ : therefore ______________________ God in your body, and in your ________________, which are God's.

SELF TEST 2

Complete I Corinthians 6:12–13 and 19–20 (each answer, 1 point).

2.023 "All things are ________________ unto me, but all things are not ________________: all things are ________________ for me, but I will not be brought under the power of any. ________________ for the belly, and the belly for ________________: but God shall ____________________ both it and them. Now the body is not for ____________________, but for the Lord; and the Lord for the ________________.

What? know ye not that your body is the ________________ of the ________________ ________________, which is in you, which ye have of God, and ye are not your own? For ye are bought with a ________________: therefore glorify God in your ________________, and in your spirit, which are ________________."

3.28 I Corinthians 6:12–13 and 19–20 give us good direction about our bodies, foods and our responsibility to spend our lives glorifying God. Memorize and recite this passage of Scripture to an adult.

"All things are lawful unto me, but all things are not expedient: all things are lawful for me, but I will not be brought under the power of any.

Meats for the belly, and the belly for meats: but God shall destroy both it and them. Now the body is not for fornication, but for the Lord; and the Lord for the body.

What? know ye not that your body is the temple of the Holy Ghost which is in you, which ye have of God, and ye are not your own?

For ye are bought with a price: therefore glorify God in your body, and in your spirit, which are God's."

SELF TEST 3

Complete I Corinthians 6:12–13 and 19–20 (each answer, 1 point).

3.028 "______________ things are ____________________ unto me, but all things are not _____________________: all things are _______________ for me, but I will not be brought under the power of any. Meats for the _______________ and the belly for _______________: but God shall _______________ both it and them. Now the _______________ is not for fornication, but for the _______________, and the _______________ for the _______________.

What? know ye not that your body is the _______________ of the Holy Ghost which is in you, _______________ ye have of ______________, and ye are not your ____________? For ye are __________________ with a _________________: therefore glorify God in your body, and in your spirit, which are ____________."

LIFEPAC TEST 3

Complete I Corinthians 6:12–13 and 19–20 (each answer, 1 point).

28. "__________ things are ________________ unto me, but all things are not ________________: all things are ______________ for me, but I will not be ______________ under the power of any. Meats for the ______________, and the belly for ______________: but God shall ________________ both it and them. Now the ______________ is not for fornication but for the ______________; and the ______________ for the ______________.

What? know ye not that your ______________ is the ________________ of the Holy ______________, which is in you, ______________ ye have of ______________, and ______________ are not your ______________? For ye are ________________ with a ______________: therefore glorify God in your ______________, and in your spirit, which are ______________."

Complete Luke 10:33–37.

1.1 "But a certain ________________, as he ________________, came where he was: and when he saw him, he had ________________ on him, And went to him and bound up his ______________, pouring in oil and __________, and he set him on his own ______________, and brought him to an ________, and took care of him. And on the morrow when he departed, he took out two ______________, and gave them to the ______________, and said to him, Take care of him; and whatsoever thou spendest more, when I come again, I will _____________ thee. Which now of these three, thinkest thou, was neighbour unto him that fell among the ______________? And he said, He that shewed ______________ on him. Then _____________ said unto him, _______, and do thou likewise."

SELF TEST 1

Complete Luke 10:33–37 (each answer, 1 point).

1.026 "But a ______________ Samaritan, as he __________________ , came where he was: and when he saw him, he had compassion on him, And went to him, and _________________ up his wounds, pouring in _______ and wine, and set him on his own beast, and _______________ him to an inn, and took care of him. And on the morrow when he __________________ , he took out two pence, and gave them to the _________________ , and said unto him, Take care of him; and whatsoever thou _________________ more, when I come again, I will repay you. Which now of these three, thinkest thou, was _______________________ unto him that fell among the thieves? And he said, He that shewed mercy on him. Then Jesus said unto him, _______ , and do thou likewise."

SELF TEST 2

Complete Luke 10:33–37 (each answer, 1 point).

2.019 "But a certain ____________________, as he journeyed, came where he was: and when he saw him, he had ____________________ on him, And went to him, and bound up his ________________, pouring in ________ and ___________, and set him on his own beast, and brought him to an inn, and took __________ of him. And on the morrow when he departed, he took out _________ pence, and gave them to the ______________, and said unto him, Take care of him; and whatsoever thou spendest more, when I come again, I will repay thee. Which now of these three, thinkest thou, was ____________________ unto him that fell among the thieves? And he said, He that shewed ______________ on him. Then Jesus said unto him, Go, and do thou ________________."

SELF TEST 3

Complete Luke 10:33–37 (each answer, 1 point).

3.022 "But a certain ________________ , as he journeyed, came where he was: and when he saw him, he had ____________________ on him, And went to him, and bound up his ________________ , pouring in oil and wine, and set him on his own beast, and brought him to an _________ , and took care of him. And on the morrow when he departed, he took out two _____________ , and gave them to the ___________ , and said unto him, Take care of him; and whatsoever thou ______________ more, when I come again, I will repay you. Which now of these three, thinkest thou, was _________________ unto him that fell among the ________________ ? And he said, He that shewed ________________ on him. Then ______________ said unto him, Go, and do thou likewise."

LIFEPAC TEST 4

Complete Luke 10:33–37 (each answer, 1 point).

40. "But a certain ________________________, as he ____________________, came where he was: and when he saw him, he had ______________________ on him, And went to him, and _____________________ up his wounds, pouring in oil and ___________, and set him on his own beast, and brought him to an _________, and took care of him. And on the morrow when he _________________, he took out two _____________, and gave them to the host, and said unto him, Take care of him; and whatsoever thou __________________ more, when I come again, I will _______________ thee. Which now of these three, thinkest thou, was ____________________ to him that fell among the _________________? And he said, He that shewed _________________ on him. Then _______________ said unto him, ________ and do thou likewise."

Complete Genesis 1:26–31.

1.1 "And God said, Let us make ______________ in our ________________, after our likeness: and let them have dominion over the _______________ of the _______________, and over the ________________ of the air, and over the ___________________, and over all the earth, and over every ___________________ thing that creepeth upon the __________________.

So God ___________________ man in his own image, in the image of ___________________ created he him; ___________________ and ___________________ created he them.

And God ___________________ them, and God said unto them, Be ___________________, and multiply, and replenish the earth, and ___________________ it: and have dominion over the ________________ of the sea, over the fowl of the _______________, and over every ___________________ thing that ___________________ upon the earth.

And God said, Behold, I have given you every ___________________ bearing seed, which is upon the face of all the earth, and every ___________________, in the which is the fruit of a tree yielding seed; to you it shall be for ___________________.

And to every ___________________ of the ___________________, and to every fowl of the ______________, and to every thing that ___________________ upon the earth, wherein there is _______________, I have given every _______________ herb for _______________: and it was so.

And ___________________ saw every thing that he had made, and, ___________________, it was very good. And the ____________________ and the _____________________ were the sixth ______________."

SELF TEST 1

Complete Genesis 1:26–28, 31a (each answer, 1 point).

1.027 "And ____________ said, Let us make ____________ in our ____________, after our ____________: and let them have ____________ over the fish of the sea, and over the ____________ of the air, and over the ____________, and over all the ____________, and over every ____________ thing that creepeth upon the earth. So God ____________ man in his own image; in the ____________ of God created he him; ____________ and ____________ created he them. And God ____________ them, and God said unto them, Be ____________, and multiply, and replenish the earth, and ____________ it: and have ____________ over the fish of the sea, and over the fowl of the air, and over every living thing that moveth upon the ____________. And God saw every thing that He had made, and, behold, it was very ____________."

SELF TEST 2

Complete Genesis 1:26–28 (each answer, 1 point).

2.030 "And God said, Let __________ make man in our image, after our likeness: and let them have dominion over the fish of the __________, and over the __________ of the air, and over the cattle, and over all the __________, and over every creeping __________ that creepeth upon the earth. So God __________ man in __________ own image, in the image of God created he him; __________ and __________ created he them. And God blessed them, and God said unto them, Be __________ and multiply, and __________ the earth, and __________ it: have __________ over the fish of the sea, and over the __________ of the air, and over__________ living thing that moveth upon the earth."

Memorize and recite these Scriptures to an adult.

3.27 Genesis 1:26–28 and verse 31a give us a clear idea of God's expectations of us in caring for the earth and for the living things on the earth.

"And God said, Let us make man in our image, after our likeness and let them have dominion over the fish of the sea, and over the fowl of the air, and over the cattle, and over all the earth, and over every creeping thing that creepeth upon the earth.

So God created man in his own image, in the image of God created he him; male and female created he them.

And God blessed them, and God said unto them, Be fruitful, and multiply, and replenish the earth, and subdue it: and have dominion over the fish of the sea, and over the fowl of the air, and over every living thing that moveth upon the earth.

And God saw every thing that he had made, and, behold, it was very good."

Complete Psalm 139:13–16 (each answer 1 point).

38. For thou hast possessed my ________________ ; thou hast ____________________ me in my mother's ____________________ . I will ___________________ thee; for I am ________________________ and wonderfully made; ____________________ are thy ____________________ ; and that my __________________ knoweth right well. My ________________________ was not ______________ from thee, when I was made in _________________ , and ________________________ wrought in the lowest parts of the earth. Thine _____________ did see my substance, yet being ____________________ ; and in thy book all my members were written, which in continuance were ___________________________ , when as yet there was ________________ of them.

Complete Colossians 3:5–8 and 12–13 (each answer, 1 point).

27. Mortify therefore your ________________ which are upon the earth; fornication, uncleanness, ________________________ affection, evil concupiscence, and covetousness, which is idolatry: For which things' sake the wrath of ______________ cometh on the ________________________ of disobedience: In the which ye also ________________ some time, when ye lived in them. But now ye also put _________ all these: ________________, wrath, malice, ____________________, filthy communication out of your mouth.

Put on therefore, as the elect of God, _____________ and ______________, ________________ of mercies, kindness, ______________________ of mind, meekness, longsuffering; Forbearing one ________________, and ________________ one another, if any man have a ________________ against any: even as _____________ forgave you, so also do ye.

Complete I Corinthians 6:12–13 and 19–20 (each answer, 1 point).

35. "All things are ________________________ unto me, but all things are not ________________________: all ________________ are lawful for me, but I will not be ___________________ under the ___________________ of any. _______________ for the ___________________, and the belly for meats: but God shall ___________________ both it and ______________. Now the ________________ is not for _______________________, but for the ________________; and the Lord for the ___________________. What? know ye not that your ________________ is the temple of the Holy ___________________, which is in you, which ye have of ______________, and ye are not your ______________? For ye are bought with a ___________________: therefore ___________________ God in your ___________________, and in your ___________________, which are ___________."

Complete Luke 10:33–37 (each answer, 1 point).

41. But a certain _______________________, as he __________________, came where he was: and when he saw him, he had _____________________ on him, And went to him, and bound up his ________________, pouring on oil and ______________; and he set him on his own __________________, and brought him to an __________, and took care of him. And on on the morrow when he ___________________, he took out two _________________, and gave them to the _______________, and said unto him, Take care of him; and whatsoever thou _____________________ more, when I come again, I will _______________ thee. Which now of these _____________, thinkest thou, was __________________ unto him that fell among the _________________? And he said, He that shewed ___________________ on him. Then ______________ said unto him, _______, and do thou likewise.

SECTION ONE

1.1 known
downsitting, uprising
path, down
ways
word, tongue
knowest
beset, before
laid, hand
wonderful, high
spirit
flee
heaven
bed, hell
wings
uttermost, sea
hand, right
darkness
night, light
hideth
night, darkness
light
possessed
mother's womb
fearfully
marvellous, soul
substance
secret, curiously
unperfect
book, written
none, them

SELF TEST 1

1.026 possessed
womb
fearfully
marvellous
substance
secret, curiously
earth
unperfect
written
continuance
none

LIFEPAC TEST 1

41. possessed
mother's womb, praise
fearfully, wonderfully
marvellous, soul
substance, hid
secret, curiously
wrought, lowest
earth, substance
unperfect, book
fashioned
none

SECTION ONE

1.1 risen
right
affection
life
appear
mortify
earth, affection
idolatry
wrath
disobedience
walked
anger
filthy, mouth
Lie, another
man
knowledge, created
Jew
bond
God
mercies, meekness
forgiving
quarrel

SELF TEST 1

1.018 Mortify, members
uncleanness
covetousness, idolatry
wrath, cometh
disobedience, ye
walked, lived
anger, malice
filthy
elect, God
beloved, mercies
longsuffering
another, forgiving
quarrel, Christ

SELF TEST 2

2.026 wrath
filthy, Lie
deeds
knowledge, him
elect, holy
mercies
longsuffering
forgiving, quarrel
forgave

SELF TEST 3

3.026 members
evil
covetousness
wrath, disobedience
walked
anger
filthy
God, beloved
kindness, meekness
forgiving
Christ

LIFEPAC TEST 2

30. Mortify, members
covetousness
wrath, disobedience
anger, malice
beloved
mercies
forgiving
Christ

SECTION ONE

1.1 lawful
lawful
belly
destroy
fornication, Lord
body
Holy Ghost
God, own
bought, glorify
spirit

SELF TEST 1

1.021 lawful
power
God, destroy
body, Lord
temple
God
bought, price
glorify, spirit

SELF TEST 2

2.023 lawful
expedient, lawful
meats
meats, destroy
fornication
body
temple
Holy Ghost
price
body
God's

SELF TEST 3

3.028 All, lawful
expedient, lawful
belly
meats, dcstroy
body
Lord, Lord, body
temple
which, God
own, bought, price
God's

LIFEPAC TEST 3

28. All, lawful
expedient, lawful
brought, belly
meats, destroy
body, Lord
Lord, body
body, temple
Ghost, which
God, ye, own
bought, price
body, God's

SECTION ONE

1.1 Samaritan, journeyed
compassion
wounds
wine, beast
inn
pence, host
repay
thieves
mercy, Jesus
Go

SELF TEST 1

1.026 certain, journeyed
bound, oil
brought
departed
host
spendest
neighbor
Go

SELF TEST 2

2.019 Samaritan
compassion
wounds, oil
wine
care
two, host
neighbor
mercy
likewise

SELF TEST 3

3.022 Samaritan
compassion
wounds
inn
pence
host
spendest
neighbor
thieves
mercy, Jesus

LIFEPAC TEST 4

40. Samaritan, journeyed
compassion
bound
wine
inn
departed, pence
spendest
repay
neighbor
thieves, mercy
Jesus, Go

SECTION ONE

1.1 man, image
fish
sea, fowl
cattle
creeping, earth
created
God, male
female
blessed
fruitful
subdue, fish
air, living
moveth
herb
tree
meat
beast, earth
air, creepeth
life, green
meat
God
behold, evening
morning, day

SELF TEST 1

1.027 God, man, image
likeness, dominion
fowl
cattle, earth
creeping
created, image
male, female
blessed
fruitful
subdue, dominion
earth
good

SELF TEST 2

2.030 us
sea
fowl
earth, thing
created, his
male
female
fruitful
replenish, subdue
dominion, fowl
every

ALTERNATE TEST 1

38. reins, covered
womb, praise
fearfully, marvellous
works, soul
frame hid
secret, curiously
eyes
unperfect
fashioned
none

ALTERNATE TEST 2

27. members
inordinate
God, children
walked
off, anger
blasphemy
holy, beloved
bowels, humbleness
another
forgiving, quarrel
Christ

ALTERNATE TEST 3

35. lawful
expedient, things
brought, power, Meats
belly
destroy, them, body
fornication, Lord
body, temple
Ghost
God, own
price, glorify
body, spirit, God's

ALTERNATE TEST 4

41. Samaritan, journeyed
compassion
wounds
wine, beast
inn
departed, pence
host
spendest
repay, three
neighbour, thieves
mercy
Jesus, Go

Health Quest

Alternate LIFEPAC Tests and Answer Keys

Draw a line under the correct answers (each answer, 2 points).

1. [**Sickness, Health, Success**] is the condition of being sound in body and mind, and free from physical disease or pain.
2. [**Bones, Organs, Cells**] are the smallest structural unit of the human body.
3. Organs are made of different kinds of [**tissues, bones, systems**] that work together.
4. Organs also work together with other organs as a [**structure, system, organ**].
5. [**Cells, Tissues, Bones**] fitted together in the shape of a skeleton give the body structure.
6. There are [**206, 260, 106**] bones in the human body that work together to form the [digestive, circulatory, skeletal] system.
7. [**Tendons, Ligaments, Joints**] attach the muscles to the bone.
8. The muscles that require conscious control are called [**voluntary, involuntary**] muscles.
9. [**Voluntary, Involuntary**] muscles such as those in the walls of your stomach and intestines work without conscious control.
10. The large intestine absorbs most of the [**air, water, waste**] from the food and some vitamins and minerals.
11. The brain works together with the [**blood vessels, chyme, spinal cord**] and nerves to form the nervous system.
12. The left side of the cerebrum controls the [**left, right**] side of the body.
13. The endocrine glands put chemicals called [**saliva, hormones, urine**] into the blood stream.
14. Hormones control [**many, all, none**] of the body's functions.
15. The pituitary gland controls and regulates all the other [**cells, organs, glands**].
16. Life begins at [**birth, conception, infancy**].
17. A baby grows for nine months in a special place inside its mother called the [**pancreas, uterus, esophagus**].
18. You are entering a stage in your life called [**puberty, old age, adulthood**].
19. Your heart almost [**shrinks, triples, doubles**] in size.
20. The right side of the cerebrum controls the [**left, right**] side of the body

Fill in the blanks with the correct answers from the list below (each answer, 2 points).

air	carbon dioxide
heart	left
oxygen	respiratory
right	upper
ventricle	villi

21. With every beat of the ____________________, gallons of blood are pumped through blood vessels that reach every cell of the body.
22. The two ____________________ parts of the heart are called the left and right atrium.
23. The two lower parts of the heart are called the left and right ____________________ .
24. Arteries work with the ____________________ side of the heart, carrying blood full of oxygen to the rest of the body.
25. Veins work with the ____________________ side of the heart to bring blood in need of oxygen back to the heart.
26. Red blood cells bring oxygen to cells and take ____________________________ away.
27. The trachea cleans the ____________________ and channels it into the lungs through two large tubes called bronchi.
28. The alveoli work to put ____________________ into the blood and remove carbon dioxide.
29. The ____________________________ system works with the circulatory system to supply oxygen to the body and remove waste from it.
30. Small, hair-like parts called ____________________ absorb nutrients from the food.

Match these items by writing the correct letter in the blank (each answer, 2 points).

31. ______ "Bad communications corrupts good manners"
32. ______ "Do all to the glory of God"
33. ______ The most important kind of growth
34. ______ Your parents are helping you prepare for this
35. ______ Should be made according to God's will
36. ______ Should be shown to the elderly
37. ______ Friends should encourage you to do this

a. Leviticus 19:32
b. physical
c. adulthood
d. spiritual
e. obey
f. respect
g. 1 Corinthians 10:31
h. 1 Corinthians 15:33
i. future plans

Complete Psalm 139:13–16 (each answer 1 point).

38. For You formed my ____________ parts; You ____________ me in my ____________ womb. I will ____________ you, for I am fearfully and ____________ made; ____________ are Your ____________ , And that my ____________ knows very well. My ____________ was not ____________ from you, When I was made in ____________ , and skillfully ____________ in the lowest parts of the earth. Your ________ saw my substance, being yet ____________ . And in Your book they all were written, The ________ for fashioned for me, When as yet there were __________ of them.

72 / 90	My Score ____________
	Adult check ____________ (Initial, Date)

social	surface	emotions
evil	protein	pore
bacteria	God's	disturbances
communicate	evaluate	

Fill in the blanks with the correct answers from the list above (each answer, 3 points).

1. Health includes a person's ____________________, social skills, mental state, and spiritual condition.
2. __________________ thoughts can be defined as those thoughts that tempt us to violate ______________ Law.
3. Discerning means being able to _________________________ information in order to judge whether it is true or not.
4. Emotions are ________________________ in the way we feel.
5. Keratin is a ____________________ found in hair and nails.
6. Pimples are formed when a tiny piece of dirt or ____________________ gets caught inside a ____________________ .
7. Bacteria on the _________________________ of the skin causes body odor.
8. ______________________ health can be defined as one's ability to get along and communicate with other people.

Answer *true* **or** *false* (each answer, 3 points).

9. __________ A person's mental and emotional condition affects their overall health.
10. __________ We are not to think about things that are praiseworthy.
11. __________ Mental and emotional health is reached by a sincere trust in one's own abilities.
12. __________ Some people have a chemical imbalance that causes them to feel extreme emotions.
13. __________ God says to use your mind to deal with your emotions.
14. __________ Being emotionally healthy helps us to be socially healthy.
15. __________ The motivating factor behind a Christian's behavior should be pride.
16. __________ Manners are commonly accepted social prejudices.
17. __________ Neighbors include only those people that live next door.
18. __________ If you honor your father and mother, God has promised to bless you.

Circle the correct answer(s) in each statement (each answer, 3 points).

19. The [**liver, skin, brain**] is the largest organ of the body.

20. You lose over [**3,000, 1,000, 100**] hairs each day.

21. Fingernails should be trimmed [**once, twice, three times**] a week while toenails should be trimmed every [**two, three, four**] weeks.

22. The thin layer of skin that covers the base of the fingernail is the [**lunula, matrix, cuticle**].

23. The strongest surface in the body is [**bone, calcium, enamel**].

24. The [**eardrum, cochlea**] is the part of the ear that helps you maintain your balance.

25. [**Nearsighted, Farsighted**] people can see close-up objects more clearly.

26. A clique is a small group of friends that [**includes, ignores, cares for**] others.

Complete Colossians 3:5–8 and 12–13 (each answer, 1 point).

27. Therefore put to death your ______________ which are on the earth; fornication, uncleanness, ______________, evil desire, and covetousness, which is idolatry. Because of these things the wrath of ______________ is coming upon the ______________ of disobedience, in which you also once ______________ when you lived in them. But now you are to put ______________ all these: ______________, wrath, malice, ______________, filthy language out of your mouth.

Therefore as the elect of God, ______________ and ______________, put on tender ______________, kindness, ______________, meekness, longsuffering: bearing with one ______________, and ______________ one another if anyone has a ______________ against another; even as ______________ forgave you, so you also must do.

82/103	My Score ______________
	Adult check ______________ Initial Date

Complete these sentences (each answer, 2 points).

body composition	cardio-respiratory endurance	cups
flexibility	lean mass	muscular endurance
strength	vitamins	water
water-soluble		

1. ____________________ makes up 60% of the body.
2. Without ____________________, carbohydrates, fats and proteins could not be changed into energy.
3. There are two types of vitamins, fat-soluble and ____________________.
4. ________________________ includes muscles, vital tissues, organs, and bone.
5. Heredity, diet and exercise determine ________________________.
6. ____ is the ability of the heart, lungs and blood vessels to deliver oxygen and nutrients to the muscles over a long period of time.
7. ____________________ is the ability to exert force for a short time.
8. ____ is the ability of a muscle or muscle group to repeatedly exert force for a long period of time.
9. ________________________ is the ability to move muscles and joint through a full range of motion.

Answer *true* **or** *false* (each answer, 2 points).

10. __________ Carbohydrates are the main building block of tissues and organs.
11. __________ Protein is found only in animal products.
12. __________ Foods that contain all the essential amino acids are called complete proteins.
13. __________ During metabolism carbohydrates are burned by cells to produce energy.
14. __________ Fat should provide more than 30% of your total calorie intake.
15. __________ Saturated fats are found in plant products.
16. __________ Unsaturated fats remain in liquid form at room temperature while saturated fats harden.
17. __________ Heart disease is caused by increased levels of cholesterol in the blood.

Circle the correct answer(s) in each statement (each answer, 2 points).

18. [**Exercise, Nutrients, Warm-ups**] supply the body with energy.

19. Essential [**amino acids, nutrients, enzymes**] include water, vitamins, minerals, proteins, fats and carbohydrates.

20 The amount of energy that a food contains can be measured by [**calories, carbohydrates, nutrients**].

21. [**Nutrients, Vitamins, Carbohydrates**] and minerals help the body change food into energy.

22. To eat to the glory of God is to be satisfied with what your body [**desires, craves, needs**].

23. Heredity, age, sex, exercise habits, diet, and lifestyle all play a part in determining our [**physical fitness, eating habits, protein intake**].

24. Aerobic means with [**effort, air, food**].

Match these items by writing the correct letter in the blank (each answer, 2 points).

25. ________ This should be included at the beginning of each workout
26. ________ This component of fitness can be built up by participating in aerobic exercise
27. ________ This exercise should be done after each workout
28. ________ Red meat, chicken, fish, nuts, and beans are included in this food group
29. ________ Ice cream, cheese, yogurt, and cottage cheese are included in this food group
30. ________ Watermelon, papaya, oranges, bananas, and lemons are included in this food group
31. ________ You need 6 or more servings of this food group each day
32. ________ This vitamin is found in fruit and it helps the body fight infection
33. ________ These vitamins are found in milk
34. ________ This a mineral that helps bones grow

a. warm-up
b. muscular endurance
c. stretching
d. bread and grain
e. calcium
f. dairy
g. fruit
h. meat and poultry
i. Vitamin C
j. Vitamins D and A

Complete I Corinthians 6:12–13 and 19–20 (each answer, 1 point).

35. "All things are __________ for me, but all things are not __________. All __________ are lawful for me, but I will not be __________ under the __________ of any. __________ for the __________, and the stomach for foods, but God will __________ both it and __________. Now the __________ is not for __________ immorality but for the __________, and the Lord for the __________. Or do you not know that your __________ is the temple of the Holy __________, who is in you, whom you have from __________, and you are not your __________? For you were bought with a __________; therefore __________ God in your __________, and in your __________, which are __________."

72/90	My Score	__________
	Adult check	__________ (Initial / Date)

Answer *true* **or** *false* (each answer, 2 points)

1. ____________ Accidents are expected and planned events.
2. ____________ A fire escape plan for your home should include two ways of escape for every room and a safe meeting place outside.
3. ____________ Never swim alone.
4. ____________ The "Good Samaritan" laws protect rescuers who are acting in good faith and are not guilty of gross negligence or willful misconduct.
5. ____________ CHECK-CARE-CALL is the correct order of emergency procedures outlined by the American Red Cross.
6. ____________ Head, neck and back injuries are never life threatening.
7. ____________ Never move a victim with a head, neck or back injury.
8. ____________ Mucus membranes trap pathogens that are airborne.
9. ____________ Getting a fever does not help fight against pathogens.
10. ____________ White blood cells attack pathogens and destroy them.
11. ____________ Vaccination works against your body's defense system.

Fill in the blanks with the correct answers from the list below (each answer, 2 points).

flammable	baking soda	fire extinguisher
kitchen	helmet	seat belt
blindness	cancer	congenital
coronary		

12. Fires most frequently occur in the ________________ .
13. Use a ____________________________ or throw ____________________________ on a kitchen fire.
14. Failure to store ________________ materials correctly can result in a fire.
15. Wear a ________________ to protect yourself from head injury.
16. Wearing a ________________________ can double your chances of surviving a car accident.
17. ____________________ heart disease is the term used for abnormalities of the heart that were present at birth.
18. ____________________ heart disease is caused by reduced blood flow to the heart resulting from closed or narrowing blood vessels.
19. ____________________ is the growth of abnormal cells on and in tissues of the body.
20. ____________________ can result from untreated diabetes.

Match these items by writing the correct letter in the blank (each answer, 2 points).

21. _______ The body's attempt at self-preservation in the case of a major injury
22. _______ All layers of the skin are damaged
23. _______ A condition that affects the whole body if a person has been exposed too long to the severe cold
24. _______ Skin turns white or grayish yellow
25. _______ Victims have red, hot skin and tiny pupils
26. _______ Caused by bacteria or a virus
27. _______ Caused by a combination of heredity, lifestyle and environment
28. _______ Tiny organisms that cause disease
29. _______ Animals that carry pathogens

a. heat stroke
b. hypothermia
c. third-degree burn
d. frostbite
e. shock
f. vectors
g. pathogens
h. non-infectious disease
i. infectious disease
j. vectors

Underline the correct answer (each answer, 2 points).

30. Talking or laughing while eating can cause [**choking, more laughter, smiles**].
31. The [**Hammer, Himmer, Heimlich**] Maneuver is one way to help a person who is choking.
32. A [**heart attack, stroke**] occurs when major blood vessels that supply the heart with blood become blocked.
33. [**CRP, MRI, CPR**] is a method of helping the heart and lungs to start working again.
34. Medications can [**relieve symptoms of, cure, vaccinate**] the common cold.
35. It takes one or two [**weeks, months, years**] to get rid of the cold virus.
36. Hepatitis is an inflammation of the [**pancreas, stomach, liver**] caused by a virus.
37. [**Antibiotics, Exercises, Cough syrups**] are prescribed to help the body fight off infection.
38. [**Doctors, Nurses, Patients**] identify diseases and disorders by examining the patient's symptoms.
39. [**Patients, Parents**] and doctors need to work together as a team.
40. Symptoms for the flu are similar to the common cold, but are [**not as bad, more severe**].

Complete Luke 10:33–37 (each answer, 1 point).

41. But a certain ____________________, as he ____________________, came where he was. And when he saw him, he had ____________________. So he went to him, and bandaged his ____________________, pouring on oil and ____________________; and he set him on his own ____________________, brought him to an ____________, and took care of him. On the next day, when he ____________________, he took out two ____________________, gave them to the ____________________, and said to him, "Take care of him; and whatever more you ____________________, when I come again, I will ____________________ you." "So which of these ________________ do you think was ____________________ to him who fell among the ________________?" And he said, "He who showed ____________________ on him." Then ________________ said to him, "__________ and do likewise."

80 / 100	My Score	______________
	Adult check	______________ Initial Date

Circle the correct answer(s) in each statement. (each answer, 2 points).

1. From ancient time, alcohol has been created by the fermentation of [**protein, sugars, water**].
2. Alcohol is a [**hallucinogen, inhalant, depressant**].
3. The effects of alcohol on the body and mind are determined by the [**amount, source, color**] that is consumed.
4. Consuming excessive amounts of alcohol in a short period of time can cause drunkenness and actually [**poison, enliven, strengthen**] the body.
5. Alcohol can cause ulcers to form in the lining of the [**stomach, lungs, throat**].
6. [**Alcohol, Tobacco, Drumming**] was first introduced to Western culture by the North American Indians.
7. Despite medical warnings, there is still a [**low, high, moderate**] number of Americans that use tobacco.
8. Approximately 50 million people smoke a total of 570 [**million, billion, thousand**] cigarettes per year.
9. [**Tar, Alcohol, Nicotine**] is directly linked to lung and oral cancer.
10. Chewing tobacco causes a [**lesser, greater**] risk of developing mouth and neck cancer than smoking.
11. Cars are the greatest cause of [**water, air, land**] pollution.
12. According to scientific theories, if enough CFC's are released into the [**ocean, soil, atmosphere**] the ozone layer will be depleted.
13. Using other means of [**transportation, exploration, pollution**] like riding your bike, can help to reduce the amount of carbon monoxide-creating engines on the road.
14. [**Hazardous, Biodegradable**] means that the waste will decompose naturally without causing harm to the environment.
15. [**Hazardous, Biodegradable**] wastes are dangerous and must be disposed of in a special manner.
16. Paper, glass, plastic and metal can be [**destroyed, recycled, decomposed**].

Answer *true* **or** *false* (each answer, 2 points).

17. __________ Intoxication occurs when small amounts of alcohol are consumed.
18. __________ Drinking coffee or some other drink containing caffeine will not rid the body of alcohol.
19. __________ Alcohol is a chemical that can have a toxic or poisoning effect on the body.

20. __________ Liver damage is a result of alcohol abuse.

21. __________ Drunkenness is not a sin.

22. __________ When someone quits smoking, they improve their health and the health of those around them.

23. __________ Cigarettes and chewing tobacco can be addicting.

24. __________ Understanding the difference between use and misuse is the key to a healthy outlook on drugs

25. __________ Taking more of a medication will always make you feel better faster.

26. __________ You cannot endanger yourself by taking another person's medication.

27. __________ Drug abuse will not lead to physical and psychological dependence.

28. __________ The abuse of a legal drug can cause physical harm and dependence.

29. __________ After Creation, God pronounced that the earth and everything in it was very good.

30. __________ The condition of the environment has no effect on its inhabitants.

31. __________ Air pollution is the presence of harmful substances in the earth's atmosphere.

32. __________ The ozone layer is contained within the troposphere.

Fill in the blanks with the correct answers from the list below. (each answer, 2 points).

body	depressants	hallucinogens
inhalants	narcotics	peace
stimulants	agricultural	atmosphere
water	cycle	conserve
soil		

33. True ____________________ and emotional stability can only come from God.

34. ____________________ slow down or reduce nerve activity.

35. Drugs can be placed into five categories: ____________________, depressants, ____________________, hallucinogens, and inhalants.

36. Christians are called to glorify God in their __________ and spirit.

37. ____________________ cause you to see, hear, and taste things that are not necessarily there.

38. ____________________ can relieve sinus congestion or give you feelings of happiness.

39. One of the easiest ways to prevent pollution of our water is to ______________________ it.

40. Water is constantly moving in a ________________ between the soil and the atmosphere.

41. Every living thing on earth needs __________________ to survive.

42. ____________________________ pollution occurs when livestock waste is not properly disposed of.

43. Water pollution not only affects the earth's water supply but also the __________________ .

70 / 88	My Score ______________
	Adult check ______________ Initial Date

ALTERNATE TEST 1

1. Health
2. Cells
3. tissues
4. system
5. Bones
6. 206
7. Tendons
8. voluntary
9. Involuntary
10. water
11. spinal cord
12. right
13. hormones
14. many
15. glands
16. conception
17. uterus
18. puberty
19. doubles
20. left
21. heart
22. upper
23. ventricle
24. left
25. right
26. carbon dioxide
27. air
28. oxygen
29. respiratory
30. villi
31. h
32. g
33. d
34. c
35. i
36. f
37. e
38. inward, covered
    mother's, praise
    wonderfully, Marvelous
    works, soul
    frame, hidden
    secret, wrought
    eyes
    unformed
    days, none

ALTERNATE TEST 2

1. emotions
2. Evil, God's
3. evaluate
4. disturbances
5. protein
6. bacteria, pore
7. surface
8. Social
9. true
10. false
11. false
12. true
13. true
14. true
15. false
16. false
17. false
18. true
19. skin
20. 100
21. twice, two
22. cuticle
23. enamel
24. cochlea
25. Nearsighted
26. ignores

278. members
passion
God
sons
walked, off
anger, blasphemy
holy, beloved
mercies, humility
another, forgiving
complaint
Christ

ALTERNATE TEST 3

1. Water
2. vitamins
3. water-soluble
4. Lean mass
5. body composition
6. Cardio-respiratory endurance
7. Strength
8. Muscular endurance
9. Flexibility
10. false
11. false
12. true
13. true
14. false
15. false
16. true
17. true
18. Nutrients
19. nutrients
20. calories
21. Vitamins
22. needs
23. physical fitness
24. air
25. a
26. b
27. c
28. h
29. f
30. g
31. d
32. i
33. j
34. e
35. lawful
    helpful, things
    brought, power, Foods
    stomach
    destroy, them, body
    sexual, Lord
    body
    body, Spirit
    God
    own, price
    glorify, body
    spirit, God's

ALTERNATE TEST 4

1. false
2. true
3. true
4. true
5. false
6. false
7. false
8. true
9. false
10. true
11. false
12. kitchen
13. fire extinguisher, baking soda
14. flammable
15. helmet
16. seat belt
17. Congenital
18. Coronary
19. Cancer
20. Blindness
21. e
22. c
23. b
24. d
25. a
26. i
27. h
28. g
29. j
30. choking
31. Heimlich
32. heart attack
33. CPR
34. relieve symptoms of
35. weeks
36. liver
37. Antibiotics
38. Doctors
39. Patients
40. more severe
41. Samaritan, journeyed
    compassion
    wounds
    wine, animal
    inn
    departed, denarii
    innkeeper
    spend, repay
    three, neighbor
    thieves
    mercy, Jesus, Go

ALTERNATE TEST 5

1. sugars
2. depressant
3. amount
4. poison
5. stomach
6. Tobacco
7. high
8. billion
9. Tar
10. greater
11. air
12. atmosphere
13. transportation
14. Biodegradable
15. Hazardous
16. recycled
17. false
18. true
19. true
20. true
21. false
22. true
23. true
24. true
25. false
26. false
27. false
28. true
29. true
30. false
31. true
32. false
33. peace
34. Depressants
35. Either order: stimulants, narcotics
36. body
37. Hallucinogens
38. Inhalants
39. conserve
40. cycle
41. water
42. Agricultural
43. soil

Health Quest

Answer Keys
Self Test Keys
LIFEPAC Test Keys

SECTION ONE

1.1 known
sitting, rising
path
down
ways
word, tongue
know
hedged, before
laid, hand
wonderful
high
Spirit
flee
heaven
bed, hell
wings
uttermost, sea
hand
right
darkness
night, light
hide
night
darkness, light
formed
mother's womb
fearfully
Marvelous
soul
frame
secret
skillfully
unformed
book, written
none
them

1.2 Adult check
1.3 Health, disease, pain
1.4 Pentathlon, five
1.5 investigate, search, pursue
1.6 Cells
1.7 building blocks (or structural units)
1.8 cells
1.9 Tissues
1.10 Organs
1.11 together, organs
1.12 skeleton
1.13 vital organs
1.14 206, skeletal
1.15 arms, legs
1.16 skull (or pelvis)
1.17 joint
1.18 Ligaments
1.19 Tendons
1.20 move, support
1.21 digest food, blood
1.22 voluntary
1.23 Involuntary
1.24 Adult check
1.25 Adult check
1.26 Adult check

SECTION TWO

2.1 f
2.2 c
2.3 j
2.4 b
2.5 i
2.6 d
2.7 h
2.8 e
2.9 a
2.10 l
2.11 g
2.12 lungs, oxygen
2.13 carbon dioxide
2.14 respiratory
2.15 Any order:
warmed, cleaned, moistened
2.16 trachea
2.17 larynx
2.18 bronchi
2.19 alveoli
2.20 "takes out the trash"
2.21 tongue
2.22 Saliva
2.23 esophagus
2.24 chyme, small
2.25 small
2.26 liver and pancreas
2.27 nutrients
2.28 water
2.29 f
2.30 c
2.31 e
2.32 b
2.33 a
2.34 Examples:
helps you think, feel emotions; controls your nervous system; controls heartbeat, breathing, digestion, muscle movement, saves you from danger
2.35 Any order:
a. cerebrum
b. cerebellum
c. brain stem
2.36 cerebrum
2.37 brain stem
2.38 cerebellum
2.39 control center
2.40 telephone wire
2.41 cerebrum
2.42 c
2.43 e
2.44 g
2.45 j
2.46 h
2.47 f
2.48 i
2.49 d
2.50 b
2.51 Adult check
2.52 Adult check
2.53 Adult check
(**Note:** Since this activity is listed as "optional," the Section II gold medal sticker may be awarded after completing activity 2.52 OR another related activity of your choice maybe substituted.)

SECTION THREE

3.1 conception
3.2 fertilizes
3.3 begins to change
3.4 nine, uterus
3.5 nine, uterus
3.6 two
3.7 five
3.8 explore the world
3.9 puberty
3.10 first
3.11 Bones, muscles
3.12 doubles
3.13 oxygen
3.14 vocal cords
3.15 hormones
3.16 responsible
3.17 friends
3.18 Evil
3.19 listen, live
3.20 Spiritual growth
3.21 God's help
3.22 Jesus Christ
3.23 child, adult
3.24 responsibilities
3.25 parents, adulthood
3.26 chores, adult
3.27 decisions (or responsibilities)
3.28 God's will
3.29 Old age
3.30 respect and honor
3.31 gray headed, old man
3.32 all men, God
3.33 Jesus Christ (or God)
3.34 glorify, enjoy
3.35 Adult check
3.36 Adult check

SECTION ONE

1.1 raised
hand
mind
life
appears
death, earth
evil desire
idolatry, wrath
disobedience
walked
anger, filthy
mouth
lie, another
man
knowledge, created
Jew
slave
God
mercies, meekness
forgiving, complaint

1.2 Adult check

1.3 true

1.4 false

1.5 false

1.6 true

1.7 (solution shown below)

1.8 b

1.9 h

1.10 c

1.11 a

1.12 d

1.13 f

1.14 e

1.15 g

1.16 extreme

1.17 first

1.18 Him, cares, Peter

1.19 Parents

1.20 encourage

1.21 help

1.22 Adult check

1.23 Adult check

1.24 Adult check

1.7

K	Z	X	E	U	I	O	O	P	D	A	S	D	F	G
T	E	R	T	F	Y	K	L	U	I	G	O	P	K	L
R	L	Z	C	V	B	N	M	K	L	O	U	I	R	E
U	Q	O	P	R	A	I	S	E	W	O	R	T	H	Y
E	W	E	V	R	T	Y	U	I	O	D	P	A	S	D
A	S	Z	D	E	A	G	F	J	K	R	L	P	T	B
C	V	B	N	M	L	I	O	H	Y	E	E	N	D	R
W	E	R	T	Y	U	Y	I	O	P	P	D	O	L	J
M	N	B	V	C	X	A	S	D	F	O	G	B	D	Q
H	P	J	E	J	U	S	T	W	B	R	V	L	O	N
P	U	E	S	D	F	G	W	X	C	T	V	E	B	N
Y	R	U	Q	Z	X	D	E	U	I	O	O	U	R	E
V	E	T	V	I	R	T	U	E	P	E	A	C	E	R
J	I	L	O	Y	E	R	C	P	R	A	I	T	T	U
K	N	O	B	L	Q	R	U	E	L	I	K	T	O	I

SECTION TWO

2.1 true
2.2 true
2.3 false
2.4 false
2.5 false
2.6 false
2.7 true
2.8. skill
2.9 when, how
2.10 listening
2.11 friend
2.12 social
2.13 love
2.14 actions
2.15 neighbor
2.16 Christian
2.17 friendly, manners, listening
2.18 demonstrate
2.19 true
2.20 false
2.21 true
2.22 true
2.23 true
2.24 false
2.25 true
2.26 God
2.27 best
2.28 friends
2.29 what is right
2.30 false
2.31 true
2.32 false
2.33 false
2.34 true
2.35 true
2.36 true
2.37 false
2.38 true
2.39 false
2.40 true
2.41 Adult check
2.42 Adult check
2.43 Adult check

SECTION THREE

3.1 true
3.2 true
3.3 false
3.4 false
3.5 true
3.6 false
3.7 true
3.8 100
3.9 300,000
3.10 Hair
3.11 Keratin
3.12 regularly
3.13 organ
3.14 Pimples, pore
3.15 Bacteria
3.16 Either order: deodorants, antiperspirants
3.17 Keratin
3.18 healthy
3.19 matrix
3.20 cuticle
3.21 c
3.22 h
3.23 d
3.24 a
3.25 b
3.26 g
3.27 e
3.28 f
3.29 enamel
3.30 root
3.31 bone-like
3.32 bacteria
3.33 Plaque
3.34 gum disease
3.35 amazing
3.36 Light, signals
3.37 television (or TV), computer
3.38 sun
3.39 Protective
3.40 farsighted
3.41 nearsighted
3.42 optometrist
3.43 g
3.44 h
3.45 f
3.46 b
3.47 d
3.48 a
3.49 e
3.50 c
3.51 Adult check
3.52 Adult check
3.53 Adult check

SECTION ONE

1.1 lawful
lawful
stomach
destroy
immorality
Lord
body
Holy Spirit
God, own
bought, glorify
spirit
1.2 Nutrients
1.3 health
1.4 nutritional
1.5 vitamins, proteins
1.6 temperature
1.7 calories
1.8 water
1.9 minerals
1.10 sugar
1.11 carbohydrates
1.12 false
1.13 true
1.14 true
1.15 false
1.16 true
1.17 sugar
1.18 Carbohydrates
1.19 metabolism
1.20 true
1.21 false
1.22 true
1.23 false
1.24 true
1.25 false
1.26 true
1.27 vitamins
1.28 balanced
1.29 Either order: fat-soluble,
water soluble
1.30 Minerals
1.31 essential
1.32 Adult check
1.33 Adult check
1.34 Adult check

SECTION TWO

2.1 a
2.2 i
2.3 e
2.4 h
2.5 b
2.6 g
2.7 j
2.8 k
2.9 c
2.10 f
2.11 d
2.12 true
2.13 false
2.14 false
2.15 false
2.16 true
2.17 false
2.18 true
2.19 true
2.20 false
2.21 true
2.22 energy
2.23 greed
2.24 health
2.25 needs
2.26 Regular meals
2.27 Adult check
2.28 Adult check
2.29 Adult check

SECTION THREE

3.1 perform
alertly, energy
meeting
endure, stress
unfit
major, health

3.2 true

3.3 false

3.4 true

3.5 false

3.6 true

3.7 false

3.8 false

3.9 true

3.10 muscles

3.11 Lean

3.12 Fat

3.13 body composition

3.14 b

3.15 e

3.16 d

3.17 c

3.18 a

3.19 four

3.20 warm-up

3.21 aerobic

3.22 muscular endurance

3.23 muscular strength

3.24 Stretching

3.25 Adult check

3.26 Adult check

3.27 Adult check

3.28 Adult check

SECTION ONE

1.1 Samaritan, journeyed
compassion
wounds
wine, animal
inn
denarii, innkeeper
repay
thieves
mercy, Jesus
Go

1.2 true
1.3 true
1.4 false
1.5 false
1.6 dangers
1.7 fire
1.8 kitchen
1.9 burns
1.10 handles
1.11 fire extinguisher, baking soda
1.12 flammable
1.13 true
1.14 false
1.15 true
1.16 false
1.17 true
1.18 true
1.19 fall
1.20 lit
1.21 slipping
1.22 ladders
1.23 toys
1.24 guns
1.25 loaded
1.26 hurt you
1.27 smelled
1.28 skin
1.29 false
1.30 false
1.31 true
1.32 true
1.33 false
1.34 Pedestrians
1.35 corners
1.36 automobile drivers
1.37 bicycle
1.38 seat belt
1.39 true
1.40 false
1.41 true
1.42 false
1.43 true
1.44 e
1.45 d
1.46 c
1.47 a
1.48 f
1.49 b
1.50 Adult check
1.51 Adult check
1.52 Adult check

SECTION TWO

2.1 true
2.2 true
2.3 false
2.4 false
2.5 true
2.6 true
2.7 false
2.8 choking
2.9 Heimlich
2.10 lie down
2.11 blocked
2.12 CPR
2.13 A stroke
2.14 should
2.15 d
2.16 e
2.17 a
2.18 c
2.19 b
2.20 true
2.21 false
2.22 false
2.23 false
2.24 true
2.25 c
2.26 d
2.27 b
2.28 a
2.29 (solution shown below)
2.30 Adult check
2.31 Adult check
2.32 Adult check

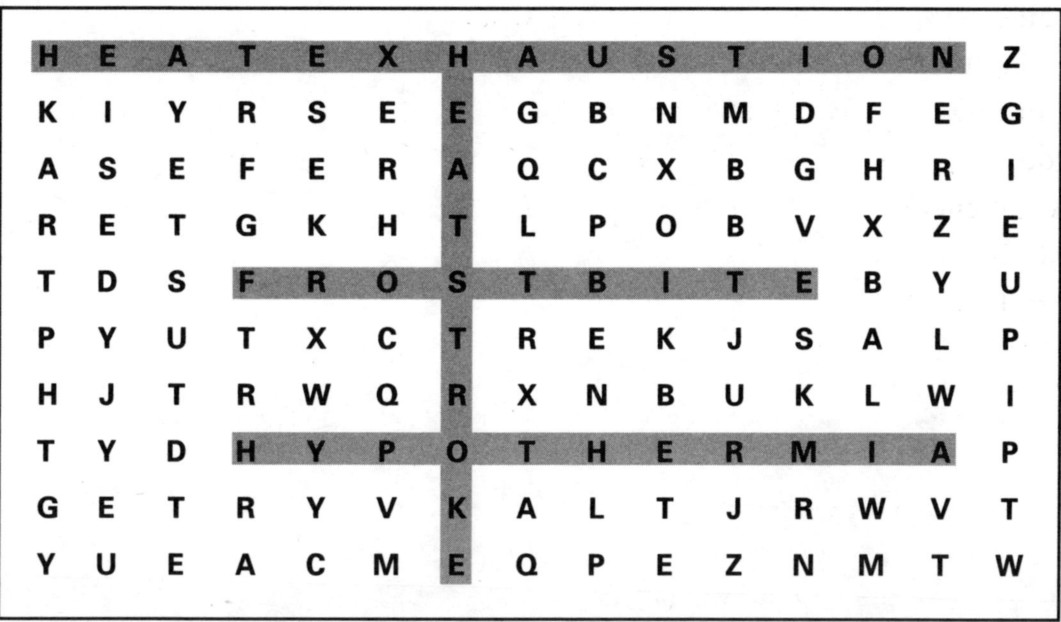

SECTION THREE

3.1 e
3.2 b
3.3 d
3.4 c
3.5 f
3.6 a
3.7 true
3.8 true
3.9 false
3.10 true
3.11 false
3.12 true
3.13 relieve symptoms of
3.14 weeks
3.15 more severe
3.16 liver
3.17 Antibiotics
3.18 Congenital
3.19 Coronary
3.20 Cancer
3.21 Either order: sarcomas, lymphomas
3.22 Diabetes
3.23 Blindness
3.24 Doctors
3.25 Patients
3.26 strengthen
3.27 glorified
3.28 good
3.29 Adult check
3.30 Adult check
3.31 Adult check

SECTION ONE

1.1 man, image
fish
sea, birds
cattle, creeping
earth, created
God
male, female
blessed, fruitful
subdue
fish, air
living, moves
herb
seed
tree
food, beast
earth, air
creeps, life
green, food
God
indeed, evening
morning, day

1.2 true
1.3 false
1.4 true
1.5 false
1.6 true
1.7 false
1.8 false
1.9 false
1.10 air
1.11 Air pollution
1.12 atmosphere
1.13 transportation
1.14 gallons
1.15 water
1.16 cycle
1.17 soil
1.18 sewage
1.19 Agricultural
1.20 diarrhea
1.21 conserve
1.22 animal
1.23 Biodegradable
1.24 Hazardous
1.25 hazardous
1.26 recycled
1.27 everyone's
1.28 Adult check
1.29 Adult check
1.30 Adult check

SECTION TWO

2.1 true
2.2 true
2.3 false
2.4 true
2.5 true
2.6 d
2.7 f
2.8 e
2.9 b
2.10 a
2.11 c
2.12 true
2.13 false
2.14 true
2.15 true
2.16 true
2.17 false
2.18 true
2.19 false
2.20 false
2.21 (solution shown below)
2.22 narcotics, stimulants
2.23 Depressants
2.24 pain
2.25 Hallucinogens
2.26 Inhalants
2.27 body
2.28 peace
2.29 Adult check
2.30 Adult check
2.31 Adult check

L	I	N	U	Y	B	G	R	D	V	Y	T	S	T	I
H	A	L	L	U	C	N	J	O	K	I	D	E	S	S
N	K	K	S	W	Z	A	Y	V	M	D	P	N	Y	T
H	A	L	L	U	C	I	N	O	G	E	N	S	L	I
R	Q	R	T	V	C	X	N	B	I	P	K	M	N	M
V	C	E	C	W	X	B	J	I	O	R	P	L	E	U
M	N	H	T	O	E	S	F	C	Y	E	O	I	J	L
U	G	I	K	L	T	B	N	T	E	S	V	C	Y	A
W	E	Q	T	R	C	I	N	B	I	S	U	M	N	N
V	C	H	Y	T	G	F	C	I	O	A	K	U	J	T
U	I	O	P	J	I	K	B	S	A	N	T	R	C	S
K	G	T	V	C	X	W	Q	B	V	T	P	I	Y	S
K	L	W	J	R	W	X	S	F	G	S	X	Z	I	O
V	I	N	H	A	L	A	N	T	S	M	N	E	R	T
H	J	C	X	O	P	E	R	U	I	N	Y	E	S	T
P	H	I	A	L	P	H	A	T	Y	Q	A	S	Y	X

SECTION THREE

3.1 Alcohol
3.2 sugars
3.3 depressant
3.4 amount
3.5 poison
3.6 Small
3.7 stomach
3.8 large
3.9 true
3.10 false
3.11 true
3.12 true
3.13 false
3.14 true
3.15 true
3.16 true
3.17 true
3.18 false
3.19 true
3.20 true
3.21 true
3.22 true
3.23 true
3.24 false
3.25 true
3.26 Adult check
3.27 Adult check
3.28 Adult check

SELF TEST 1

1.01 disease
1.02 Pentathlon
1.03 smallest
1.04 Organs, tissues
1.05 different
1.06 together
1.07 Bones, structure
1.08 protect
1.09 bones, skeletal
1.010 Ligaments
1.011 attach, muscles
1.012 Muscles
1.013 voluntary
1.014 Involuntary
1.015 bones
1.016 cells
1.017 organs
1.018 joint
1.019 heart
1.020 g
1.021 c
1.022 b
1.023 f
1.024 a
1.025 e
1.026 inward
womb
fearfully
Marvelous
frame
secret
skillfully, earth
unformed
written
days
none

SELF TEST 2

2.01 blood vessels
2.02 atrium
2.03 ventricle
2.04 Arteries
2.05 right
2.06 Red blood cells
2.07 mouth
2.08 trachea
2.09 alveoli
2.010 circulatory
20.11 Saliva
2.012 chyme
2.013 nutrients
2.014 large intestine
2.015 waste
2.016 excretory
2.017 kidneys
2.018 urine
2.019 nerves
2.020 cerebrum
2.021 left, cerebrum
2.022 right, cerebrum
2.023 brain stem
2.024 hormones
2.025 Hormones
2.026 pancreas, blood
2.027 skeletal, muscular
2.028 pituitary
2.029 Endorphins
2.030 respiratory
2.031 thyroid
2.032 excretory
2.033 digestive
2.034 nervous
2.035 endocrine
2.036 circulatory

SELF TEST 3

3.01 disease
3.02 smallest
3.03 Organs
3.04 together
3.05 Bones
3.06 bones, skeletal
3.07 muscles
3.08 voluntary
3.09 involuntary
3.010 fertilizes
3.011 nine months, uterus
3.012 more slowly
3.013 puberty
3.014 Bones, muscles
3.015 doubles
3.016 oxygen
3.017 puberty
3.018 obey
3.019 Spiritual
3.020 Jesus Christ
3.021 adult
3.022 parents
3.023 decisions
3.024 the will of God
3.025 blood vessels
3.026 atrium
3.027 ventricles
3.028 Arteries
3.029 Veins
3.030 Red blood
3.031 trachea
3.032 alveoli
3.033 circulatory
3.034 honor
3.035 Jesus Christ
3.036 glorify, enjoy
3.037 corrupts
3.038 d
3.039 a
3.040 b
3.041 e
3.042 h
3.043 c

SELF TEST 1

1.01 Health
1.02 mental, emotional
1.03 think, affects
1.04 trust, God
1.05 extreme
1.06 Lord
1.07 parents
1.08 true, noble, just, pure, lovely, good, meditate
1.09 Evil
1.010 Discerning
1.011 general revelation
1.012 God's Word
1.013 consequences
1.014 Emotions
1.015 Christians
1.016 mind
1.017 Pastors
1.018 death, members
uncleanness
covetousness, idolatry
wrath, coming
disobedience, you, walked
lived
anger, malice, filthy
elect, God, beloved
mercies
longsuffering, another
forgiving, complaint
Christ

SELF TEST 2

2.01 different
2.02 Social
2.03 very important
2.04 personality
2.05 listen
2.06 Communication
2.07 speak
2.08 know
2.09 friend
2.010 social
2.011 Christian
2.012 b
2.013 c
2.014 e
2.015 g
2.016 d
2.017 h
2.018 f
2.019 a
2.020 i
2.021 true
2.022 true
2.023 false
2.024 true
2.025 false
2.026 wrath
filthy
lie
deeds
knowledge, Him
elect, holy
mercies
longsuffering
forgiving, complaint
forgave

SELF TEST 3

3.01 Health
3.02 God's
3.03 Discerning
3.04 disturbances
3.05 Keratin
3.06 Pimples, pore
3.07 Bacteria
3.08 communicate
3.09 true
3.010 false
3.011 false
3.012 false
3.013 false
3.014 true
3.015 true
3.016 true
3.017 false
3.018 false
3.019 three
3.020 eardrum
3.021 middle
3.022 cochlea
3.023 impulses
3.024 Wax
3.025 destroy
3.026 members
desire
covetousness
wrath, disobedience
walked
anger
filthy
God, beloved
kindness, meekness
forgiving
Christ

SELF TEST 1

1.01 true
1.02 false
1.03 true
1.04 true
1.05 false
1.06 false
1.07 Proteins
1.08 animal
1.09 complete
1.010 Carbohydrates
1.011 metabolism
1.012 Fats
1.013 essential
1.014 water
1.015 metabolism
1.016 cups
1.017 vitamins
1.018 balanced
1.019 water-soluble
1.020 regulate
1.021 lawful
power
God, destroy
body, Lord
temple
God
bought, price
glorify, spirit

SELF TEST 2

2.01 true
2.02 true
2.03 true
2.04 true
2.05 true
2.06 j
2.07 d
2.08 g
2.09 b
2.010 f
2.011 c
2.012 i
2.013 a
2.014 e
2.015 nutrients
2.016 30%
2.017 Allowances
2.018 two
2.019 animal
2.020 Unsaturated
2.021 Saturated
2.022 increased
2.023 lawful
helpful, lawful
Foods
foods, destroy
sexual
body
temple, Holy Spirit
price
body, God's

SELF TEST 3

3.01 Nutrients
3.02 nutrients
3.03 calories
3.04 Vitamins
3.05 health
3.06 needs
3.07 physical fitness
3.08 with
3.09 true
3.010 false
3.011 false
3.012 true
3.013 true
3.014 true
3.015 false
3.016 false
3.017 true
3.018 warm-up
3.019 Muscular endurance
3.020 Stretching
3.021 meat and poultry
3.022 dairy
3.023 fruit
3.024 bread and grain
3.025 Vitamin C
3.026 Vitamins D and A
3.027 Calcium
3.028 All, lawful
helpful, lawful
stomach
foods, destroy
body
Lord, Lord, body
temple
whom, God
own, bought
price
God's

SELF TEST 1

1.01 false
1.02 true
1.03 false
1.04 false
1.05 true
1.06 true
1.07 false
1.08 true
1.09 true
1.010 false
1.011 true
1.012 c
1.013 e
1.014 d
1.015 b
1.016 a
1.017 f
1.018 fall
1.019 ladders
1.020 toys
1.021 loaded
1.022 hurt
1.023 smelled
1.024 tornado
1.025 Earthquakes
1.026 certain, journeyed
bandaged, oil
brought
departed
innkeeper
spend
neighbor
Go

SELF TEST 2

2.01 true
2.02 true
2.03 true
2.04 false
2.05 true
2.06 true
2.07 true
2.08 choking
2.09 Heimlich Maneuver
2.010 blocked
2.011 CPR
2.012 Shock
2.013 third-degree burn
2.014 Movement
2.015 Hypothermia
2.016 Frostbitten
2.017 Heat stroke
2.018 Heat stroke
2.019 Samaritan
compassion
wounds, oil
wine
care
two, innkeeper
neighbor
mercy
likewise

SELF TEST 3

3.01 Chicken pox
3.02 Infectious diseases
3.03 Non-infectious diseases
3.04 Pathogens
3.05 b
3.06 d
3.07 a
3.08 c
3.09 pathogens
3.010 pathogens
3.011 Vaccination
3.012 Antibodies
3.013 false
3.014 false
3.015 true
3.016 true
3.017 false
3.018 true
3.019 false
3.020 true
3.021 true
3.022 Samaritan
compassion
wounds
inn
denarii
innkeeper
spend
neighbor
thieves
mercy, Jesus

SELF TEST 1

1.01 false
1.02 false
1.03 true
1.04 false
1.05 true
1.06 false
1.07 false
1.08 true
1.09 atmosphere
1.010 transportation
1.011 Air pollution
1.012 air
1.013 animal
1.014 everyone's
1.015 Hazardous
1.016 Biodegradable
1.017 recycled
1.018 hazardous
1.019 Sewage
1.020 conserve
1.021 diarrhea
1.022 soil
1.023 gallons
1.024 Agricultural
1.025 cycle
1.026 water
1.027 God, man, image
likeness, dominion
birds
cattle, earth
creeping
created, image
male, female
blessed
fruitful, subdue
dominion
earth
everything

SELF TEST 2

2.01 c
2.02 f
2.03 d
2.04 g
2.05 e
2.06 a
2.07 b
2.08 true
2.09 true
2.010 false
2.011 false
2.012 false
2.013 true
2.014 true
2.015 true
2.016 true
2.017 true
2.018 true
2.019 false
2.020 peace
2.021 instructions, expiration
2.022 Any order: swallowing, injection, inhalation, absorption
2.023 Either order: narcotics, stimulants
2.024 Inhalants
2.025 body
2.026 Hallucinogens
2.027 Depressants
2.028 pain
2.029 emotional, God
2.030 Us
sea
birds
earth, thing
created, His
male
female
fruitful, fill
subdue, dominion
birds
every

SELF TEST 3

3.01 poison
3.02 sugars
3.03 large
3.04 amount
3.05 depressant
3.06 Small
3.07 stomach
3.08 Alcohol
3.09 true
3.010 true
3.011 false
3.012 false
3.013 false
3.014 true
3.015 true
3.016 true
3.017 true
3.018 true
3.019 true
3.020 true
3.021 true
3.022 true
3.023 Smoking
3.024 nicotine, carbon monoxide and tar
3.025 1960's
3.026 greater
3.027 Tobacco
3.028 high
3.029 Tar
3.030 billion

1. e
2. f
3. h
4. l
5. m
6. n
7. d
8. a
9. c
10. i
11. o
12. g
13. b
14. j
15. k
16. q
17. disease
18. Pentathlon
19 puberty
20. first
21. Bones, muscles
22. responsibilities
23. oxygen
24. vocal cords
25. Organs, tissues
26. 206, skeletal
27. muscles, voluntary
28. conception
29. attach, muscles
30. pancreas, blood
31. skeletal, muscular
32. pituitary
33. Endorphins
34. respiratory
35. thyroid
36. excretory
37. digestive
38. nervous
39. endocrine
40. circulatory
41. inward
    mother's womb
    praise, fearfully
    wonderfully
    marvelous, works
    soul
    frame, hidden
    secret
    skillfully, wrought
    lowest, earth
    substance
    unformed, book
    fashioned
    none

1. matrix
2. Evil
3. Discerning, true
4. disturbances
5. Keratin
6. Pimples, pore
7. Bacteria
8. Social, communicate
9. true
10. true
11. true
12. false
13. true
14. false
15. false
16. true
17. true
18. false
19. God
20. the Lord
21. speak
22. friend
23. bacteria
24. social
25. obey
26. best
27. friends
28. 100
29. treated with respect
30. death, members
    covetousness
    wrath
    disobedience
    anger
    malice
    beloved, mercies
    forgiving
    Christ

1. balanced
2. nutrients
3. calories
4. muscular strength
5. health
6. needs
7. physical fitness
8. 13
9. true
10 false
11. false
12. true
13. true
14. true
15. false
16. true
17. a
18. e
19. h
20. g
21. k
22. i
23. c
24. b
24. j
26. d
27. f
28. All, lawful
helpful, lawful
brought, stomach
foods, destroy
body
Lord, Lord, body
body, temple
Spirit, whom
God, you, own
bought, price
body, God's

1. false
2. true
3. true
4. true
5. true
6. true
7. true
8. true
9. true
10. true
11. false
12. true
13. true
14. true
15. true
16. ladders
17. loaded
18. tornado
19. Heimlich Maneuver
20. blocked
21. Shock
22. Movement
23. Hypothermia
24. Frostbitten
25. Heat stroke
26. White blood cells
27. Antibodies
28. Chicken pox
29. Infectious diseases
30. Non-infectious diseases
31. Pathogens
32. g
33. d
34. a
35. h
36. c
37. e
38. b
39. f
40. Samaritan, journeyed
    compassion
    bandaged
    wine, inn
    departed
    denarii
    spend
    repay
    neighbor, thieves
    mercy, Jesus
    Go

1. sugars
2. depressant
3. poison
4. 1960's
5. high
6. billion
7. Tar
8. inhabitants
9. gases
10. stratosphere
11. water
12. true
13. false
14. false
15. true
16. false
17. false
18. false
19. true
20. true
21. false
22. false
23. true
24. true
25. false
26. true
27. true
28. Depressants
29. Hallucinogens
30. peace
31. drug
32. Medication
33. Prescription
34. air
35. Hazardous
36. high
37. atmosphere
38. transportation
39. animal
40. Biodegradable
41. recycled
42. Inhalants
43. body
44. pain
45. 100
46. soil
47. diarrhea
48. conserve
49. Small
50. Alcohol
51. nicotine, carbon monoxide and tar
52. Smoking